SCHOOL

CW00860342

Designed by Val Carless
Cover design by Robert Perry

KINGFISHER
An imprint of Larousse plc
Elsley House,
24-30 Great Titchfield Street,
London, W1P 7AD

First published by Larousse plc 1996

A CIP catalogue record for this book is available from the
British Library

ISBN 0 7534 0077 4

Kingfisher

2

3

Timetable

	Mon.	Tues.	Weds.	Thurs.	Fri.
8am					
9am					
10am					
11am					
noon					
1pm					
2pm					
3pm					
4pm					
5pm					

Do you bring your P.E. kit to school on the wrong days? Do you forget when you have Art? Here's a timetable for you to fill in to help you remember!

PUNCTUATION POWER!

CAPITAL LETTERS

Capital letters are used:

- At the beginning of sentences:
  Look at that!

- For names of:

people	Plug
places	Beanotown
days	Monday
countries	America
languages	English

- For the personal pronoun 'I'
  Do I need that?

COMMON MISTAKE ✕
Using capital letters in the middle of a sentence or a word.
I Don't thiNk you should do tHat ...!

FULL STOPS

Sentences usually end with either a full stop, question mark or exclamation mark:

- Statements usually end with a full stop.
  I see what you mean.

- Questions end with a question mark.
  Do you understand?

- An exclamation mark is used to show a forceful comment or a joke.
  What a laugh!

COMMAS

- Used to separate items in a list.
  Yesterday I bought a new pair of training shoes, a baseball cap and a bat.

- Used before direct speech.
  Plug said, "I want to be a model."
  "You mean a plasticene® one," joked Smiffy.

COMMON MISTAKE ✕
Using, too many, commas, in a, sentence, is, a, common mistake.

APOSTROPHES

- Used to show possession (that something belongs to somebody).
  Gnasher's bone.
  Walter's cuddly toy.

- Used to contract two words into one.
  Walter's a softy.

COMMON MISTAKE ✗
Using apostrophes for plurals:
Fish and Chip's.
Bash Street Kid's

SPELLING

Many find spelling difficult. There are several ways to improve your spelling.

WRITE IT DOWN

Spellings have patterns – we are good at remembering patterns. So, if you are not sure of a word, try writing two or three possible spellings. Which looks right?

USE A DICTIONARY

If you think you know how the word starts, look it up in a dictionary.

LOOK FOR WORD FAMILIES

Words are usually grouped in families:

```
          ize
author ─── ity
          ization
```

This family consists of four words. In all of them *author* is spelled the same. Look for families and spelling becomes easier (e.g. realize, reality and realization).

SOME SPELLING RULES

There are several spelling rules. If you learn the rules, you'll learn the spellings!

Making plurals (more than one).

- Usually just add s:
  comic   *comics*

- Words that end in an s, add es.
  class   *classes*

- Words that end in x or z, add es.
  fox   *foxes*
  buzz   *buzzes*

- Words that end in y. If the letter before the y is a vowel, add s.
  donkey   *donkeys*

- If the letter before the y is a consonant, the y becomes *ies*.
  lady   *ladies*

- Words that end in o usually add s.
  piano   *pianos*

- Some add es:
  tomato   *tomatoes*
  potato   *potatoes*

- Words that end in sh and ch add es.
  flash   *flashes*
  church   *churches*

- Words that end in f or fe change to ve and add s.
  shelf   *shelves*
  wife   *wives*
  Except:
  beliefs   chiefs
  gulfs   roofs

- Words that stay the same:
  deer   sheep

7

SENTENCES

There are four main types of sentence.

- Statement:
  I like the Beano.
- Question:
  Do you understand?
- Command:
  Give it to me.
- Exclamation:
  Look at that!

Sentences usually contain a VERB.
Billy Whizz **runs** fast.

Statements, questions and exclamations normally contain a SUBJECT. The subject tells us who or what the sentence is referring to.
I like to read.
Who is **that?**

There can also be an OBJECT. This comes after the verb in statements. The object is the thing or person that is affected by the verb.
I spilt the **milk**.
Do you like **The Beano?**

VERBS

A verb shows what a person or a thing is doing.
I am **running**.
I am **laughing**.

NOUNS

Nouns are names for a person, a place or a thing:
biscuit, comic, Plug, Bash Street Kids, Dundee.

ADJECTIVES

Adjectives are words that describe something. They work with nouns.
A **funny** person.

ADVERBS

They make verbs and adjectives clearer or stronger. With adjectives – they usually end in *ly*.

ENGLISH

COLLECTIVE NOUNS

This is the term given to the names of a group of things.

A shrewdness of apes
A herd or pace of asses
A cete of badgers
A sloth or sleuth of bears
A flock or flight of birds
A sounder of wild boar
A herd or gang of buffalo
A clowder or glaring of cats
A brood of chickens
A murder of crows
A litter of cubs
A herd or mob of deer
A pack or kennel of dogs
A herd of elephants
A business of ferrets
A cloud of flies
A skulk of foxes
A gaggle of geese
A herd of giraffes
A flock or herd of goats
A siege of herons
A stud of horses
An exaltation of larks
A leap of leopards
A rookery of penguins
An unkindness of ravens
A chattering or murmuration of starlings

A _____ of flies

A _____ of wild boar

A _____ of penguins

A _____ of leopards

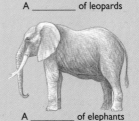

A _____ of elephants

USEFUL INFORMATION

MULTIPLICATION TABLES

	2	3	4	5	6	7	8	9	10	11	12
2	4	6	8	10	12	14	16	18	20	22	24
3	6	9	12	15	18	21	24	27	30	33	36
4	8	12	16	20	24	28	32	36	40	44	48
5	10	15	20	25	30	35	40	45	50	55	60
6	12	18	24	30	36	42	48	54	60	66	72
7	14	21	28	35	42	49	56	63	70	77	84
8	16	24	32	40	48	56	64	72	80	88	96
9	18	27	36	45	54	63	72	81	90	99	108
10	20	30	40	50	60	70	80	90	100	110	120
11	22	33	44	55	66	77	88	99	110	121	132
12	24	36	48	60	72	84	96	108	120	132	144

WEIGHTS AND MEASURES

LENGTH

10 mm	1 centimetre
100 cm	1 metre
1,000 m	1 kilometre

AREA

100 sq mm	1 sq centimetre
110,000 sq cm	1 square metre
10,000 sq m	1 hectare

WEIGHT

| 1,000 g | 1 kilogram |
| 1,000 kg | 1 tonne |

VOLUME

| 1,000 cu cm | 1 cubic decimetre |
| 1,000 cu dm | 1 cubic metre |

ROMAN NUMERALS

1	I	7	VII	13	XIII	19	XIX
2	II	8	VIII	14	XIV	20	XX
3	III	9	IX	15	XV	50	L
4	IV	10	X	16	XVI	100	C
5	V	11	XI	17	XVII	500	D
6	VI	12	XII	18	XVIII	1,000	M

TEACHERS

It is useful to remember that all teachers were once the same age as you. Difficult to believe, I know, but it's true. So bearing this in mind, just think that they also:

Teachers are a fact of life. Like toothache and colds and flu - you're definitely going to experience them. So get used to it and just put up with them!

- *Lied about not doing homework.*
- *Stayed at home in bed instead of going to school.*
- *Got bad results in exams and tests.*
- *Got into trouble.*

So when they're moaning at you, just remind them that they weren't so good at school either!

WHAT TEACHERS SAY	WHAT THEY MEAN
You can't do your best work, if you're noisy!	*Shut up, I've got a headache!*
It'll be better for you all if the person who did this owns up.	*I haven't got a clue who did it, but when I find out who it was they're dead!*
Okay, what did we do last lesson?	*I can't remember.*
Do you think I like having to tell you off and moan at you all the time?	*I love telling you off and moaning at you all the time.*
Have you done the homework I set you?	*I hope not then I can moan at you*

TEACHER TYPES

MAD DICTATOR TYPE
Distinguishing features:
Moustache
(even the women).
Tweed suits or tweed
dresses.
Hates:
Children. Other teachers
(especially young ones and
drama teachers).
Likes:
Shouting. Giving detentions
and homework.
Common sayings:
Sit down!
Children need discipline.
HINTS
Try to avoid this type of
teacher. If you do come
across them, do not speak
out of turn.

HIPPY TEACHER
Distinguishing features:
Badly fitting jacket or
flowery dress.
Shoes that need cleaning
or open-toed sandals.
Hates:
Having to tell someone off.
Shouting.
Likes:
Folk music, wildlife,
animals, trees.
Common sayings:
Please everyone, be
quiet...please...please...
Oh, okay, you can talk.
HINTS
Buy a good revision book
and do all your work
at home.

TRENDY TEACHER

Distinguishing features:

Earring if male.

Nose ring (male and female).

Designer label clothes.

Hates:

Anyone telling them to grow up and act their age.

Likes:

Anything that's 'in'.

Common sayings:

Okay, guys, settle it…

Do you need this hassle: do I need this hassle…?

HINTS

This teacher wants to be liked and accepted as 'one of the gang'. Smile and nod at them.

THE NEWLY QUALIFIED TEACHER

Distinguishing features:

Smart appearance (trying to impress everyone).

Jacket or suit.

Clean shoes.

Hates:

Getting up early.

Staying late to do marking.

Likes:

Teaching – remember they have only just qualified.

Children (same reason as above).

Common sayings:

Er, would you mind doing the work…please?

HINTS

You can undermine a new teacher's confidence, by saying, 'Our old teacher never did that'.

Teachers aren't the most important people in your school. You must also get on with these members of staff. Try to get them to like you – it will make your school life a lot easier!

CARETAKER

Wears:
Old brown or blue overall with patches. Boots (usually with odd coloured laces).

Habits:
Always carries a broom. Moans about litter. Claims that children were better behaved in the old days.

Hates:
Children. Anyone who messes up their floors.

DINNER LADIES

Do you want ketchup on your yoghurt or custard on your burger? Be nice and polite to them!

SECRETARIES

The secretaries make sure you are sorted out, so it is always best to stay in their good books.

TIPS ON AVOIDING SCHOOL

> Ever feel as though you don't want to go to school? Need to stay in bed, watch videos and try and get the highest score on your computer game?

Don't skive – you'll get caught.

It's best if you get off school with your parents' permission.

Prepare a bowl of muesli the night before. Put water in and leave it to soak overnight. Next morning…run to the toilet.

When parents are in earshot make loud retching noises as though you were being sick. Throw muesli down the loo. Shout down to parents:

"I've just been sick. Come and look!"

If they do look, they won't look for long!
Extra acting bit.
Lower your eyelids and breathe heavily. Occasionally pretend to burp.

AVOIDING HOMEWORK
Do not try these excuses:
- The dog ate it.
- My mum used it as a nappy for the baby.
- I dropped it in a puddle.
- An alien stole it.

These are terrible excuses and have been used by your teacher, their teacher and your teacher's teacher's teacher.

Try this brilliant letter. It can be used time and time again!

Make a photocopy of the following letter.

When you are asked for your homework, hand the letter to your teacher with the words:

"I think this should explain everything".

No.10 Downing Street
London

To Whom it May Concern

The bearer of this letter has been involved in a
most secret operation for the government of
Great Britain.

It has been a highly dangerous mission that
will have taken many hours. The mission is still
in progress: please do not risk its failure by giving
the bearer of the letter a detention, any extra
homework or any other form of punishment.

World peace depends upon this.

Thank you.

Mercy

The Prime Minister

PS If you follow these instructions, I'll make
    sure that you are remembered in the New
    Year's Honours List.
PPS If you don't, a couple of large men in black
    raincoats will be paying you a visit very soon.

BEST AND WORST...

MY FAVOURITE TEACHER

Name
Nickname
Subject taught
Description
Height
Colour of hair
Colour of eyes
Clothes usually worn
Favourite sayings
Habits
Why you like him/her
Marks out of ten

MY WORST TEACHER

Name
Nickname
Subject taught
Description
Height
Colour of hair
Colour of eyes
Clothes usually worn
Favourite sayings
Habits
Punishments given out by
him/her
Why you don't like him/her
Marks out of ten

TEACHERS AND LESSONS

Fill in the following to find out just how much time you have to spend with teachers.

HOW MANY HOURS PER YEAR DO YOU SEE YOUR TEACHER?

A How long does a lesson last? (in minutes)

B Number of lessons per week in which you see the teacher.

C MULTIPLY A and B

This gives you how many minutes a week you will see that teacher.

The average number of weeks you spend at school (in a year) is 39.

D MULTIPLY C by 39
This gives you how many minutes you will see the teacher in a year.

E DIVIDE D by 60 (minutes in an hour)
This gives you how many hours you will spend in that teacher's company.
Frightening hey!

> **N.B.** *You may be lucky and spend less time than this as teachers go to meetings, skive off and are ill.*

HANDWRITING...

Graphology is the study of handwriting. Some experts think that a person's handwriting reveals hidden secrets about their feelings, thoughts and personalities.

Ask your friends to give you a sample of their handwriting. It should be on plain paper, with no lines or margins.

THINGS TO LOOK FOR

There are several general things to look for.
Is the handwriting:

- Neat or messy?
- Large or small?
- Strong or weak?

These may show whether a person is organized or not.

MARGINS

A wide left margin

wide margin

Indicates a lively personality

A narrow left margin

narrow margin

Indicates a shy person
If there are wide *and* narrow margins, the person may be unreliable!

The neater the writing, the more logical the person.

HORIZONTAL LINES

These are the lines that go across the page.

- **Straight across** Points to a reliable person.
- **Lines going up** Suggests the writer is optimistic.
- **Lines going down** May show that a person is unhappy.

straight across
Shows a stable person

sloping up
Shows a hopeful outlook

sloping down
Shows someone who looks on the bad side

straight writing
Shows confidence

forward slant
Shows an easy-going nature

backward slant
Shows a shy nature

SLANT

This means whether the letters in the words are straight or lean to one side.

● **Straight** Suggests a logical and independent person.

● **Forward slant** Indicates a friendly, sociable person. Too slanted may show someone who exaggerates.

● **Backward slant** This can show someone who finds it hard to show their feelings.

SIZE

● **Large writing** This can show that the writer is a lively, outgoing person. If it is very large though, it can show selfishness and vanity!

● **Small writing** The writer could be modest. They show great attention to detail.

SPACING

The spacing between words should be between the width of an 'n' or an 'm'.

● **Narrow word spacing** The writer could be very sociable, with lots of friends.

● **Wide word spacing** Can show shyness. Or maybe they just like being on their own!

Large writing
Shows an outgoing personality

small writing
Shows a patient nature

narrow spacing
Likes to keep people close by

wide spacing
Likes to keep people at a distance

23

DOTTING 'i's AND CROSSING 't's

I Just the way a person writes an 'i' or a 't' can reveal an awful lot about their personality!

- Dotted to the left.

  a cautious person

  Shows a lack of care or a cautious person.

- Dotted to the right.

  to the right

  Indicates fast writing and a person with so many ideas that they want to get them down quickly.

- Connected to the next letter.

  it's joined up

  This could show that a person is intelligent and has a logical mind.

  A circle instead of a dot shows that a person might be untrustworthy and immature!

- t crossed in same position.

  attention to detail

  Shows a careful person who pays attention to detail.

- A low t bar.

  a low t bar

  Suggests a shy, self-conscious person.

- A short t bar.

  a short t bar

  Can mean that a person is cautious.

A downward sloping t bar can indicate that the person is unhappy, while an upward sloping one shows a happy, lively person.

t If a writer doesn't ever cross their ts, they are probably lazy or don't pay attention to detail!

YOUR SIGNATURE

This is the greatest statement about you that your writing can show. It tells who you are and what you think about yourself. It should be compared with your normal handwriting. If it is bigger, it suggests that you feel good about yourself. A small signature might mean that you are a timid person.

Sign your name here

WHOSE WRITING IS THIS?

Match the handwriting to the Bash Street Kid you think wrote it!

A

B

C

D

Answers:
A. Smiffy
B. Wilfrid
C. Fatty
D. Spotty

25

27

Before schools were invented children learned from their families.

ANCIENT SCHOOLS

THE ANCIENT EGYPTIANS

It was important to be able to read and write in Ancient Egyptian society. If a person could do this, they could become a priest or a scribe and work for the government.

When they reached the age of five, boys from rich families attended a writing school. These were run by priests

Egyptian schoolchildren sat cross-legged on the ground.

who were very strict and would often beat lazy boys. Pupils learned to write by copying out picture symbols called *hieroglyphs* from exercise books. They chanted the meanings of words and phrases aloud.

Egyptian schoolchildren wrote with reeds and twigs on pieces of stone and broken pottery. Only when the boys could write well were they allowed to write on papyrus which was an early type of paper.

THE ANCIENT GREEKS

According to the famous philosopher Aristotle, Greek schoolchildren had to take their learning seriously. He wrote:

"Education certainly ought not to be a means of amusement. Young people are not playing when they are learning, because all learning is painful."

Perhaps this still applies nowadays!

LEARNING IN A GYMNASIUM

Greek boys started going to school between the ages of six and seven. The school was called a *gymnasium*. Children who attended were sons of wealthy freemen and lessons had to be paid for. Children from poorer families either didn't go to school or left at a young age.

Greek girls didn't go to school. They were taught to cook and look after the house.

The Ancient Greeks believed that education should enrich the body and the mind and turn people into model citizens. So school children had lessons in citizenship as well as reading, writing, dancing, singing, music and sports.

RIGHTING WRONG WRITING

Greek pupils wrote on waxed tablets with a stick called a stylus. If they made a mistake, they simply rubbed it out and began again with a clean surface!

I PREFER CRAYONS!

THE ROMANS

RIDICU-LUDUS FACT

The Roman name for school was ludus, which means play!

The Romans liked all things to do with Ancient Greece. They were so impressed by Greek schools that they decided to open some of their own. As a result, hundreds of schools were set up in Ancient Rome.

EARLY LEARNING

The children who went to school started at about the age of seven. They were taught how to read and write and do simple sums using an abacus. Only children with poorer parents went to school. Richer children were taught at home by a tutor.

SPEAKING PUBLICLY

At about the age of 12 some Roman children went to a higher school where they received lessons from a tutor called a *grammaticus*. They studied Roman literature. They would also be taught the skills of oratory (speaking in public), which was incredibly important if a child wanted to go into the law or develop a career in politics.

Those who weren't rich enough to have personal tutors or attend schools would follow their father's trade, learning the skills needed from him. Some would learn military skills and become a soldier in one of the Roman army's great legions.

EDUCATION EQUALS MONEY!

Slaves who could read or write were considered to be highly desirable goods and could be sold for incredible prices. Some were sold for around three quarters of a million sesterces, which at today's prices would buy a brand new Mercedes sports car!

THE VIKINGS

Viking children were very lucky – they didn't have to go to school, because there weren't any! But, like most good things, there was a drawback. Their parents had to teach them.

Viking children were taught skills that would help them survive. Girls were taught to cook, sew, look after the cattle and hoe and weed fields. They were also taught how to handle weapons and to defend themselves when the men were away.

Boys were taught how to fish, sail, ride, forge iron and tan leather. They also learned how to use weapons.

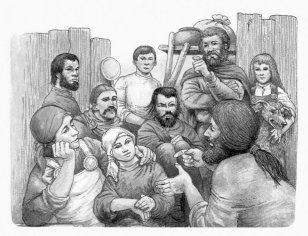

Children and adults learned by listening to stories that usually told of heroic acts and adventures.

THE AZTECS

Aztec children were expected to be hardworking, honest and obedient. Although they didn't go to school when they were young, all children were taught to respect their elders and help with the household chores.

STUDYING RELIGION

At the age of 15, a boy could go to one of two different types of school: the *Calmecac* or the *Telpochcalli*.

Children from noble families tended to go to the Calmecac where they could study religion (the Aztecs worshipped over 60 gods), Aztec history, law, mathematics and writing. They were taught by priests or noble elders called *Conservators*.

Girls were expected to run the home and, unless they came from a noble family, they didn't go to school. Most girls needed to know how to weave and spin cloth and cook.

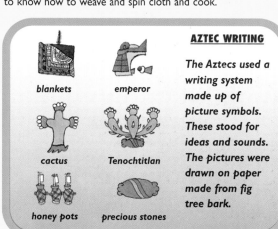

AZTEC WRITING

blankets

emperor

cactus

Tenochtitlan

honey pots

precious stones

The Aztecs used a writing system made up of picture symbols. These stood for ideas and sounds. The pictures were drawn on paper made from fig tree bark.

SCHOOLS IN BRITAIN

MIDDLE AGES

In the Middle Ages elementary schools were run mainly by priests and monks. These were usually the only people who could read Latin which was the official language of the Church.

HENRY VIII

Between 1536 and 1540, Henry VIII closed down most of the monasteries after a big disagreement with the Pope. Because

lots of schools were run by monks and priests this meant that many elementary schools also closed down.

Only a few grammar schools were left, so Henry and his son Edward VI had to build some more!

VICTORIANS

Who introduced compulsory schooling for children?
The Victorians!

In 1880, the British Government made it law that all five to ten year olds had to go to school. As if that wasn't bad enough, in 1890, they raised the school leaving age to 12!

MODERN SCHOOLS

The school leaving age is now 16.

All children between the ages of five and sixteen have to go to school and are entitled to a free education.

There has been a great deal of change in education in the 20th century – children have moved from writing on slates to using word processors.

GIRLS' EDUCATION

You may have noticed that girls haven't been mentioned much in this history of schools. This is because girls were usually taught at home and learned to cook, sew, clean houses and have babies!

King James I of Britain refused to let his daughter learn Latin as he said:

"To make women learned and foxes tame has the same effect: to make them more craftier."

If a girl did receive any sort of education in olden times, it was probably because she came from a rich family. But even this was sometimes thought strange. During the 18th century, educated and intelligent women were made fun of and called 'blue stockings'.

Schools for girls began to be set up, but they tended to teach girls subjects like sewing, dancing, cooking, music and etiquette – the sort of skills they would 'need' to become good wives.

Luckily this approach to girls' education has nearly disappeared in the Western world and girls and boys are taught the same subjects.

Greek girls were taught household skills by their mothers.

PUNISHMENTS

For thousands of years, pupils have been punished by teachers for misbehaving or acting in a way that their teachers don't like. History is littered with teachers who have got up in a grumpy mood and taken it out on their poor students.

HERE'S HOW TO MAKE WRITING LINES EASY!

The Ancient Egyptians were very strict teachers. They didn't take any nonsense. Anyone stepping out of line was flogged as an example to the others!

The Ancient Greeks thought that punishment was important to develop a person's character. They thought it was a good idea to 'knock' sense into their pupils, and floggings were common.

Roman teachers also thought whippings were a good idea and if someone got the answer wrong, a flogging would make sure they got it right the next time!

But however hard the Romans and Greeks appeared, the Aztecs made them look like softies. If an Aztec student fell asleep, the teacher woke them up by pricking them with cactus spines! Very badly behaved children were made to breathe the smoke of hot chillies being burned on an open fire. It was a good idea for an Aztec child to pay attention in class!

SCHOOL DINNERS

OOPS! THE CURRY'S A BIT HOT!

ROMAN DINNERS

Roman school children took their own food to eat at dinner time. A typical meal would consist of: bread, olives, cheese, dried figs, nuts and cold water. This might not sound fantastic, but it was (and still is) an incredibly healthy diet.

VIKING DINNERS

The Viking diet consisted of eating a lot of fish: raw, pickled, smoked, dried, salted – you name it, they had a way of eating it. Vikings loved sausages that were made with a little meat, and lots of lard and blood!

In Tudor and Elizabethan times, school kids could drink beer! However, it was nothing like the beer we know today. It probably tasted like stewed socks and wasn't particularly strong in alcohol content.

Victorian school kids could look forward to a brilliant meal of gruel, salt beef and bread. They might even get a bit of cheese if they were really lucky.

After World War II, free school meals were given to many children in Britain. These were supposed to give a healthy balanced diet. Now school dinners in Britain give children a choice. Some children even phone their local takeaway and have a meal delivered to the school.

AZTEC DINNERS

Aztecs ate corn pancakes called tortillas, filled with beans, tomatoes and chillies. They were also fond of eating human flesh – arms and legs were often added to stews and the palm of a hand was supposed to be particularly delicious.

OTHER SCHOOLS

Can you guess how many different types of school there are in Britain? Two, three, four...? You must be kidding! There are lots!

Infant

Junior

Combined Infant & Junior

Middle

Comprehensive

Grammar

Secondary Modern

Direct Grant

Church School

Grant Aided

Secondary schools with sixth forms

Secondary schools without sixth forms

Sixth Form College

Community School

City Technology College

Special School

College of Further Education

College of Higher Education

Voluntary College

Private School

Independent

Non-maintained school

Preparatory schools

All those schools: frightening hey?

YOU DON'T HAVE TO GO TO SCHOOL TO LEARN!

Some children in Britain have private tutors and don't go to school at all. The tutors visit their houses and teach them on a one-to-one basis. There are several reasons for this, the main one being that parents decide that they don't want to send their children to a school. Another reason is the fact that some children misbehave so badly at school that they get suspended and aren't allowed to attend! Because it is the law that every child under the age of 16 should have an education, these children have to be taught at home.

HOSPITAL SCHOOLS

What would happen if you were ill and had to spend a lot of time in hospital? You'd think that people would feel a bit sorry for you and let you off your schoolwork, wouldn't you? No chance!

Many hospitals in Britain have their own education unit, complete with teachers and books for you to work from in your hospital bed! They usually organize work for you from your ever-so-kind teachers at school, then help you with it! These hospital teachers have to teach children of many different ages, so they receive special training for teaching a wide age range.

Even being ill and lying in a hospital bed isn't a good enough excuse for missing schoolwork! It just doesn't seem fair, does it?

OUTBACK SCHOOLS

Not being able to get to a school isn't a good enough reason to miss learning in some countries. Australia is a huge country with vast areas of desert and almost uninhabited areas called the outback. For the few children who live in this region, special lessons have to be set up.

In the outback, there aren't enough children of the same age to be able to teach in 'same age classes'. And, because the children live so far apart, it would be impossible to bus them to a nearby large school as it could be hundreds of kilometres away!

YOU'RE MEANT TO SIGN MY PLASTER, SOFTY! NOT DO SUMS ON IT!

Some children in the outback talk to their teachers by radio.

LEARNING BY RADIO

There are hundreds of 'outback' schools that have about ten pupils and two teachers. The children are all aged from five to sixteen and the teachers have to teach every subject.

Another way of learning in the outback is by radio and television. The Australian Broadcasting Corporation broadcasts programmes for children who cannot go to school and have to stay at home to learn. Schoolwork is also sent through the post to pupils and they do it at home. Children get in contact with teachers, who are hundreds of kilometres away, using CB radios. This way of learning has a lot of advantages – for instance you can't get into trouble for being late for school – as you're there already! You could also claim that your homework got lost in the post or the radio reception was so bad that you thought that there wasn't any homework that week!

TOO MANY KIDS...

Schools around the world are quite different from most schools in Britain. In places like Singapore, schools operate a two session school day. Some pupils attend school from 7.30 am until 1.00 pm when they go home. Other pupils then arrive for the afternoon session which lasts from 1.05 pm until 6.35 pm. This is because there are so many children and not enough school buildings for them! This also happens in Far Eastern countries.

SATURDAY SCHOOL

After a hard week at school many people love to have a Saturday morning lie in. But, for some children this doesn't happen as they have to get up and go to school!

Japanese children often have extra school lessons.

44

Some French schoolchildren have Wednesday afternoons off, but then have to attend school on Saturday mornings. It is also a common practice in British public schools for pupils to attend Saturday morning lessons. This is because many schools use Wednesday afternoons for sports.

SIX-DAY WEEK

In other countries, children also go to school on days that we reserve for resting and playing.

In Islamic countries pupils attend school from Sunday to Thursday as Friday is the Islamic day of prayer. Some pupils in China get an even worse deal – they only get Sundays off and have to go to school six days a week!

But when you are feeling hard-done-by about having to do your homework, think about school children in Japan. Education is so important in Japan that many Japanese children get home from their normal schools then go to another school in the evenings and weekends! These schools are called *Juku* and specialize in helping children to pass exams. It is thought to be a huge disgrace for a child to fail exams in Japan, as they will not be able to get a good job after leaving school. This pressurized examination system is known as *Juken Jigoku*. This means examination hell!

46

TEACHER'S TEST

So, you thought you could get away with skimming through this book! Here's a quick test to see if you've been paying attention.

What kind of beans did the Aztecs eat?
Human beans.

What happened to the cross-eyed teacher?
He couldn't keep his pupils under control!

What's a Greek urn?
About 20 drachmas!

What do you call a young Viking with a sore throat?
A little Norse!

Why was the pharaoh so sad?
Because he couldn't find his mummy.

Why are there no more cannibals?
Someone ate them all!

Where are the kings and queens of Britain crowned?
On the head.

Why are the Middle Ages sometimes called the Dark Ages?
Because there were so many knights.

What exams do farmers take?
Hay-levels!

Use 'centimetre' in a sentence:
'My sister was walking home and I was centimetre.'

What did Caesar say when he was stabbed?
"Ouch!"

Which car is like a classroom?
A model-T Ford – it has little nuts inside and a crank up front!

Why are fish so well educated?
Because you always find them in schools!

SCHOOL REPORT

Name ....

Form ....

ENGLISH

Shall I compare you to a Summer's Day? No, you are beyond that! You thoroughly deserved the Cooker Prize for literature. GradeA+++++++++++++

MATHS

Your brilliant thesis has rightly been awarded the 'Noblest Prize'. By completely destroying Pythagoras' theory, you have transformed geometry as we know it.
Mark: $\sqrt{A} = \int \Delta \, \pi \, 2 \times 105$

SCIENCE

I think Einstein would have been reduced to a gibbering wreck by your genius. Good luck with your PhD.
Mark: $E = mc^2$

PE

I look forward to seeing you compete in the next Olympic Games where you are sure to win at least ten golds. Marks: Get set, go!

FRENCH

Très très très très très très très très très très très très très très très très très très très très bien! Mark: Dix out of dix

COOKERY

Your banquet for the assembled heads of state at Buckingham Palace was a masterpiece - a poem in food. Mark: Michelin 5 stars

HEAD'S REPORT

The most brilliant scholar I have ever encountered! You are magnificent and should be rewarded for being so wonderful.

PHOTOCOPIABLE SCHOOL REPORT

Worried about taking your latest school report home? Don't be! Simply photocopy this report and fill in your own name. Give it to your parents and wait to be showered with heaps of praise.